BECKET

AN ILLUMINATION OF THE LIFE AND DEATH OF THOMAS BECKET

OLIVER POSTGATE
& NAOMI LINNELL

Kingfisher Books

Kingfisher Books, Grisewood & Dempsey Ltd,
Elsley House, 24–30 Great Titchfield Street,
London W1P 7AD

First published in 1989 by Kingfisher Books

BRITISH LIBRARY CATALOGUING IN PUBLICATION DATA

Postgate, Oliver.
  Becket: an illumination of the life and death of
Thomas Becket
  1. England. Becket, Thomas, Saint. 1120?–1170
  I. Title.   II. Linnell, Naomi
  942.03'1'0924

ISBN 0-86272-405-8

Phototypeset by Rowland Phototypesetting Ltd
Bury St Edmunds, Suffolk
Colour separations by Newsele Litho SpA, Italy
Printed by Vallardi Industrie Grafiche SpA, Italy

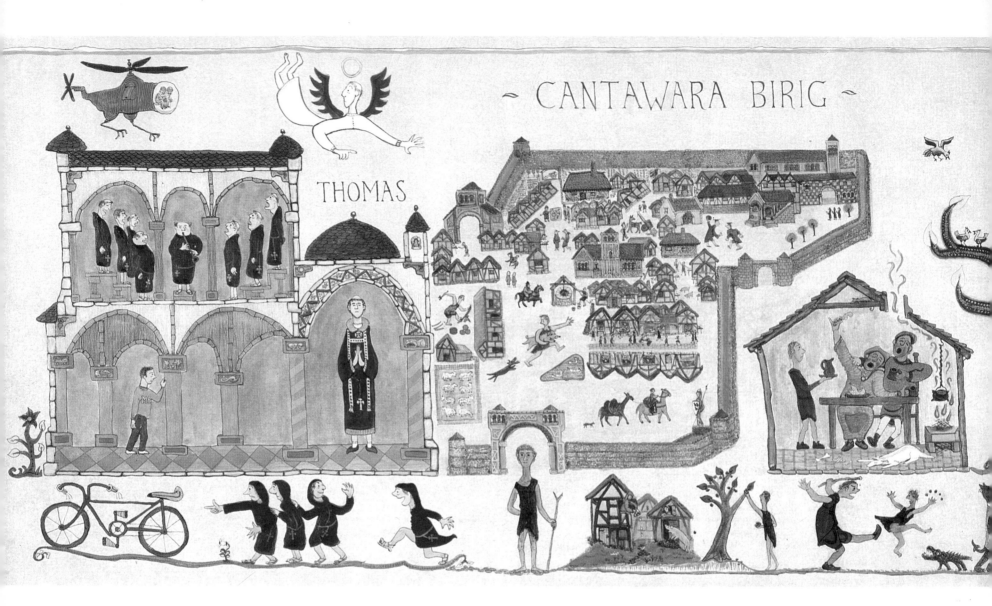

THOMAS

**I**f you go and stand in the crypt of Canterbury Cathedral, you will be standing near where Thomas Becket stood, over eight hundred years ago.

Mind you, the city outside was quite different in those days. The main centre was a huddle of small wooden houses in narrow smelly streets. If you had been born at that time you would

WHAT SHALL IT PROFIT A MAN?

CREDO CREDIMUS

probably have been skinny, dirty and very quick on your feet. But Canterbury was not a poor city. It was the centre of the English Church and the home of rich merchants and scholars.

Although there was no Social Security, the poor did quite well because rich people gave them money, not so much out of pity as to make sure that they would have a place in Heaven.

People also made lavish gifts to the Church, which became so rich and powerful that it claimed the right to judge its own people. So any person who could claim a connection with the Church could, if they broke the law, be tried in a Church Court. There they would get a fairly light punishment and any fines would go to the Church, not into the king's treasury.

INTERDICT

We may wonder why the king put up with this. He certainly did not like it but, like everybody else, he wanted to go to Heaven when he died. So he was very careful not to offend the Pope who could, if he wished, 'excommunicate' the king, or worse, lay an 'interdict' on the whole of his kingdom. That would be terrible, like taking away everybody's 'ticket to Heaven'.

Thomas Becket was born in about 1120. His parents were wealthy Norman merchants who lived in London. They sent him to school in Surrey and later to college in Paris.

As a young man, Thomas went into the service of Theobald, Archbishop of Canterbury. He did well, and when Henry II was crowned in 1154, Theobald recommended Thomas to him.

The king liked Thomas and made him his Royal Chancellor. They became very great friends and more or less ran the country together. The Church was displeased with Thomas because he used his position to make sure the Church paid its proper share of the king's taxes, which was something it always tried to avoid doing. In 1161 Archbishop Theobald of Canterbury died.

Theobald had wanted Thomas to be the next archbishop so that he could guard the Church's privileges. Henry wanted Thomas because he thought he would help him to take them away.

The bishops and the monks did not think much of Thomas because he was not even a monk. He was just a 'king's clerk' and had been a soldier. But, as usual, the king had his way.

Once he was Archbishop of Canterbury, Thomas turned his back on his friend the king and did all he could to prevent the king taking away the Church's privileges. The king prepared a document called the Constitutions of Clarendon which would take away the Church's sole right to try its own people. Thomas refused to put his seal to it and had to flee to France.

Thomas went straight to Pope Alexander III, who was living in France. He asked him to make Henry give up the Constitutions and invite him back, but the Pope was an exile himself and could not do this because he needed Henry's support. So Thomas had to stay in exile for years, hoping that Henry would one day do something that the Pope would not be able to forgive.

In 1170 Henry did this. He had the Archbishop of York crown his eldest son, Prince Henry, King of England. The Pope had forbidden this, so it was an insult to him as well as Thomas.

Henry, realizing that he had gone too far, came to France to meet Thomas and make friends again. Their meeting was joyful. Henry gladly reinstated Thomas and gave him back his lands.

Later Thomas heard that his lands in Kent were not being given back but were being stripped of their stock by one of Henry's officers, Ranulf de Broc. He asked Henry to go back with him to England and make a new start together, but Henry would not go. So Thomas went back alone and received a great welcome in Canterbury. But the Church in the rest of England was not so

pleased to hear of his return, especially when he excommunicated the bishops who had taken part in the illegal coronation as well as the de Broc family who had been plundering his estates.

Then Thomas started on a ceremonial tour of England on his way to greet the new young king. Meanwhile the unhappy bishops went to complain to Henry at Bures, in France.

At Bures, the Archbishop of York told Henry that Thomas had raised an army and was going through the country threatening people with excommunication if they did not support him.

This was not true but Henry did not know that. He lost his temper and shouted at his court: "What idle treacherous knaves you are that you let your king be mocked by a low-born clerk!"

Henry soon recovered his temper and, with his council, decided to send a deputation to Canterbury to invite Thomas to visit the young king at Winchester to swear allegiance to him.

Thomas would have been happy to do this but he did not get the chance. Four of Henry's barons had already left for England to capture Thomas and take him as a prisoner to Winchester.

During the afternoon of December 29th, 1170 the four barons with the de Brocs and a company of soldiers, rode into the courtyard of Thomas's palace in Canterbury. The four barons hung their armour on a mulberry tree and went in to talk to Thomas. They had a terrible row and stormed out to put on their armour. Thomas's servants slammed the front door behind them.

The barons beat on the door and shouted while inside the palace Thomas's clerks and monks were very frightened. Then the barons climbed on to a roof and began to break their way in.

Thomas's monks picked him up from his chair, carried him down through the cellars of the palace and out into the cathedral cloisters. There they made a procession and entered the dark

cathedral. The barons were not far behind. They shouted for Thomas at the door of the cathedral and Thomas showed himself. They came in and had another shouting-match. Then three of the barons tried to lift Thomas and put him on to the back of the other one, who was not wearing armour, so that they could carry him out of the cathedral. That did not work out.

Thomas was too strong and too angry. There was a brawl. Suddenly Thomas knelt and prayed. One of the barons swung his sword and cut the top off Thomas's head. Then they rode away.

Robert de Broc told the monks to get rid of the body quickly or he would have it thrown on the dump. Some of the monks thought Thomas was a king's clerk who had got what he deserved

but none of them wanted that to happen to him. So they carried his body down into the crypt. There they took off his robes and found that underneath them he was wearing a monk's habit.

This caused them great joy. But it was nothing to the joy they felt when they found under the habit a hair shirt and pants—full of fleas and lice trooping away from the body as it cooled.

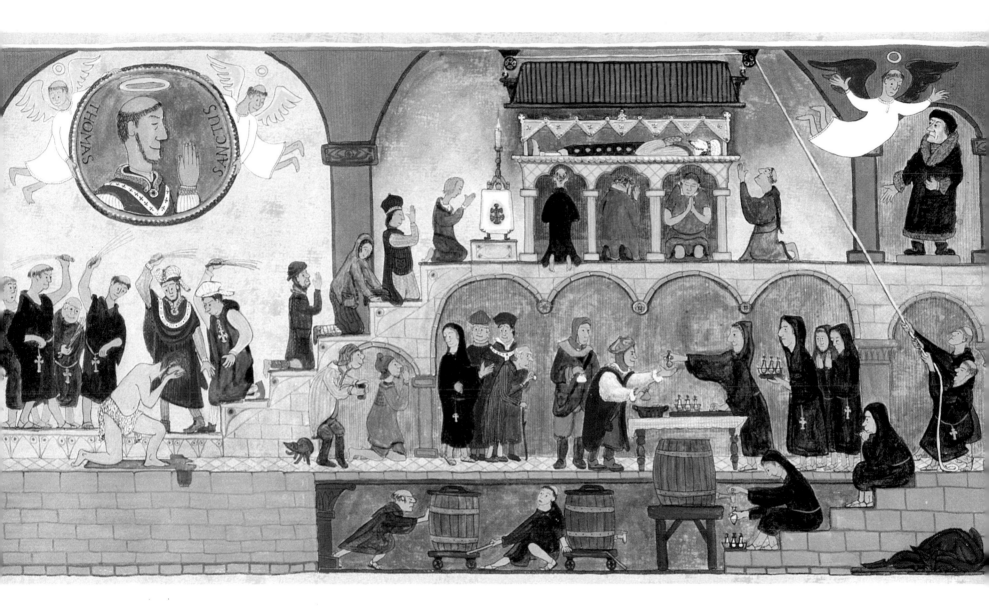

This discovery proved beyond doubt that Thomas and everything about him was utterly holy. Henry gave up his quarrels with the Church and came barefoot to do penance and be beaten.

Thomas had won. He was made a saint and for the next three hundred years thousands of pilgrims came to pray at his tomb and bring gifts for the Church—which became very rich indeed!

23

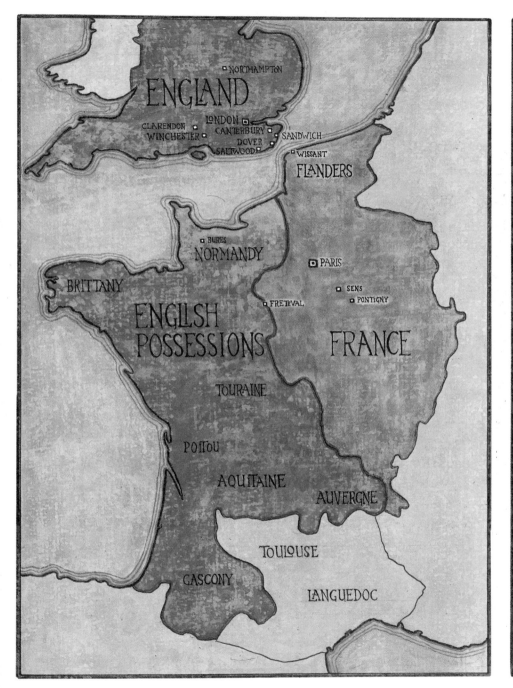

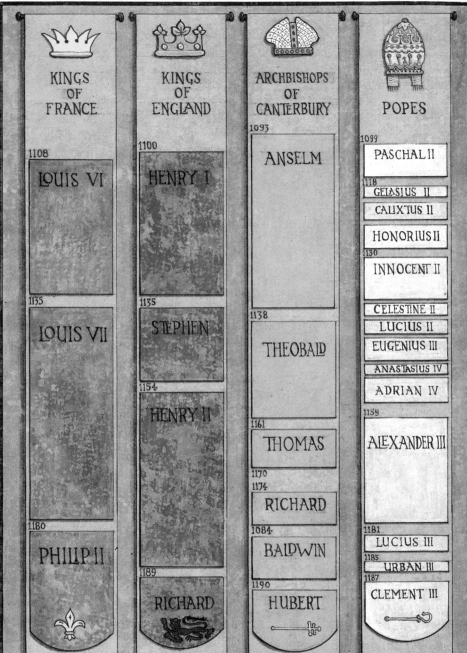

KINGS OF FRANCE	KINGS OF ENGLAND	ARCHBISHOPS OF CANTERBURY	POPES
1108 LOUIS VI	1100 HENRY I	1093 ANSELM	1099 PASCHAL II
			1118 GELASIUS II
			CALIXTUS II
			HONORIUS II
			1130 INNOCENT II
1135 LOUIS VII	1135 STEPHEN	1138 THEOBALD	CELESTINE II
			LUCIUS II
			EUGENIUS III
			ANASTASIUS IV
			ADRIAN IV
	1154 HENRY II	1161 THOMAS	1159 ALEXANDER III
		1170	
		1174 RICHARD	
1180 PHILIP II		1084 BALDWIN	1181 LUCIUS III
			1185 URBAN III
	1189 RICHARD	1190 HUBERT	1187 CLEMENT III

24

THE LIFE AND DEATH OF THOMAS BECKET

When we try to imagine what life was like in twelfth century England, we naturally find ourselves imagining what life would be like for us if we were suddenly taken back to that time.

We would find it very strange to be deprived of television and lavatories, but of course the people who lived then did not feel a bit deprived, because those things had not been invented.

If you had been born in about the year 1120, the child of ordinary peasants in a country village, you would come into a simple world in which almost everybody spent their lives in hard work just in order to stay alive.

Perhaps the strangest thing for us to understand is that the idea that you were free—that you were your own person—would probably never occur to you.

Everybody belonged to, and served, somebody else.

You would be your parents' child of course. But your parents probably belonged to the lord of the manor and had to earn the right to live by working in his fields.

The lord of the manor was also somebody's man. He held the village from his lord, who was probably a Norman baron, and he, in his turn, held the whole area from his lord, the king. The king quite simply thought he owned everything, lands, houses, people, pigs—the lot!

This was the basis of the feudal system, a piece of organized exploitation by which the wealth and ease of the Norman land-holders and the king was earned by the hard work of the poorest people in the kingdom.

Today we would think this very unjust, and so it was, but that is no reason to assume that the people were unhappy. For them, happiness was a good harvest, a roof that didn't leak, home-brewed ale to drink and, most important of all, a good lord to serve, because a good lord would honour another feudal duty, which was to protect and care for his people.

Life in a country village was hard but very simple, predictable and, in a very unsafe world, fairly secure.

If a village lad were suddenly to come—by good or bad fortune—to a sophisticated city like Canterbury, he would be astonished and alarmed.

Come to think of it, so would we!

First of all there was the smell. That must have been very astonishing.

The main centre of the city was the huddle of wooden buildings and narrow unpaved streets around the cathedral. There were over a hundred shops in Canterbury but they were not like the shops we know. Each shop was about two metres wide and, seen from the street, it was no more than a wooden flap that hinged down from a hole in the house wall, perhaps with a picture-sign hung over it.

Inside the houses the goods were prepared; bread was baked, shoes were made, beer brewed, mutton-fat boiled up to make candles. Each trade would have its own street. Some of the street names are still there today.

Some trades, like slaughtering animals for meat, took place in the muddy streets and the unwanted bits of the carcases were left for the dogs and the pigs and the chickens, all of which wandered about loose, to pick over as they rotted. There was no running water and no drains, only, when it came, the blessed rain.

The lad would see people using money quite freely. He might never have handled money and he probably only knew the value of the crude coins in terms of farm produce—that a chicken was worth a penny, for

instance and that it was quite usual for chickens to be specified and given as rent for land.

But what would have made our lad most uneasy would be the sense of isolation. He had left his village and was in the middle of this busy mass of people. They seemed to be going about their business knowing what they were doing and who they belonged to, while he was not only alone, he did not know whose person he was.

Perhaps he would have gone, with other beggars and cripples, to the cathedral gate. Persons of wealth and rank would come by there and hand out alms—small coins mainly—to the poor and needy.

The rich may have done this out of pity, but they also did it to earn the favour of God. If you were rich and wanted good things for yourself, it was only prudent to give generously to the poor and to the Church, so as to make sure there would be a place for you in heaven.

Having no money or possessions, our lad would not have been worth murdering or robbing, so he was probably not in much danger, but if he did happen to get mixed in any trouble, if he were accused of stealing, for instance, the king's justice could be very rough.

In this respect any people who could claim to have any connection with the church were lucky, because the Church maintained that it had the right to judge its own people. It claimed that they were not subject to the king's law but only to the laws of the Church.

cross God's steward on earth, the Pope, he would risk being 'excommunicated'. That would cut him off from God's mercy and all Christians would be forbidden to have anything to do with him. If the Pope was really offended he could lay an 'interdict' on the whole of the kingdom. If that were to happen it would mean that Mass could not be said, babies could not be baptised and the dead could not be buried according to the rites of the Church. That would be like taking away their 'ticket to heaven', and that was something that everybody, from serfs to kings, dreaded more than death itself.

But our lad knew nothing of such perils. Being sensible he would probably have gone home to his village but if he couldn't do that he might well have gone to the kitchens of some merchant or craftsman and run errands in return for bits of food. With luck he would become part of the household and if, for instance, his master was Gregory the Moneyer, who made coins, he might eventually be able to say that he was 'Gregory's man'. Then he would know who he was and begin to feel safe again.

Of course there is no record of what happened to our village lad because he is the creation of our imaginations, but we do know quite a lot about Thomas Becket and what happened to him.

So the Church held its own courts and judged its own people. Its punishments were never as severe as those of the king's courts and the fines it levied on 'criminous clerks', as they were called, went to the Church and added to its wealth, not into the king's treasury.

When we remember what absolute rulers the Norman kings were, how they saw themselves as being owners of everything, we may wonder why they put up with this situation for a minute.

They certainly did not like it, but there were good reasons for putting up with it. The Church and the state ran the country together, the king through the force of laws and customs and the Church through its moral laws and codes of behaviour. The Church's laws were in some ways more effective in keeping the peasants hard-working, humble and hopeful. If you disobeyed the king's laws you might get away with it, but if you disobeyed God's laws, God would know and then you might not go to Heaven.

Also, the king, like everybody else, had a lord. He held his land by the grace of God and he too expected to answer to God for the way he had protected and nourished God's Church. He knew that if he were to

Although Thomas was born into the same world as our rural lad, what he saw of it must have been quite different.

He was born on December 21st, probably in the year 1120. His father, Gilbert Becket, was a prosperous Norman merchant living in London.

Not much is recorded of Thomas's early life. There are only glimpses, like snapshots in a family album.

His mother, Matilda, was very devout. She always saw to it that when her son went out he took with him items of food and clothing to give away to the poor. She was keen on education and probably arranged for a local priest or scholar to teach him his letters at home.

When he was about ten he went as a boarder to an Augustinian Priory at Merton in Surrey and later to one of the London grammar Schools, probably St Paul's.

We have a glimpse of Thomas in his late teens becoming attached to a Norman nobleman, Richer de l'Aigle, who was an aristocrat and a keen sportsman. Encouraged perhaps by Richer, Thomas went to study in Paris. Little is known about his time there.

We know that Thomas's education came to a sudden end when his mother died and soon we see him working for a merchant banker called Huit-deniers (eightpence). It is said that Gilbert Becket's trade had fallen on hard times, perhaps as a result of one of the many fires that swept through the thatched wooden houses of the city.

At the age of about twenty-four, through his father's influence, Thomas entered the service of Theobald, Archbishop of Canterbury, as a clerk.

Incidentally, in the twelfth century the word 'clerk' was used to describe any sort of scholar or lettered person, especially those connected with the Church. Thus a bishop who had done something illegal would be described as a 'criminous clerk'.

Theobald had quite a number of clerks because it was the custom for young men to go into the service of important people as they would go to university today, to learn and study as they served.

Thomas was said to be charming and light-hearted but a bit ostentatious in his dress. He may also have been a bit of a 'climber', a bit pushy in the way he tried to attract his master's attention at the expense of the other clerks. We are told that his fellow-clerks, who included Roger of Pont l'Eveque, called him 'Baille-hache', which means: 'The hatchet man'. This may be no more than idle gossip but we do know that Roger, who later became archbishop of York, seems to have been Thomas's enemy for most of his life.

At some time during this period Thomas must have.

decided or realized that his life was to be spent in the service of God. Such a life could be very strict. For Thomas it meant an exact programme of prayers and services as well as regular 'scourgings', which were beatings given by other priests as a punishment for sins.

Theobald recognized Thomas's ability and sent him to Auxerre and Bologna to study law, and in 1154 arranged for him to take 'holy orders' as a deacon so that he could become Archdeacon of Canterbury.

In the same year Henry Duke of Normandy, who already ruled over large areas of western France, became King Henry II of England.

Archbishop Theobald, thinking no doubt that it would be a good idea to have one of his own people close to the king, recommended Thomas to his service. The king liked him and appointed him Royal Chancellor.

Up till then Thomas's life has been successful but not extraordinary. Now, one might say, the fun began.

The post of Royal Chancellor was not great. It was not much more than Royal Chaplain and chief clerk but in Thomas's time it became great, because he and the king became very close friends and worked together, sharing the running of the country.

In this way Thomas became a powerful man. He also became very rich. He received a large income from rents that came to him as Archdeacon of Canterbury and Royal Chancellor. He received presents from people who wanted his favour and, most important of all, lavish gifts of land and goods from the king.

The extravagance and magnificence of Thomas's household became a legend and its grandeur rivalled that of the king himself, who did not mind a bit because Thomas was 'his man'.

Tales are told of their friendship; of how the king, pitying a cold beggar, wrestled with Thomas for his new fur-lined cloak, took it off his back and gave it to the beggar. We are told how Henry would arrive at Thomas's hall at dinner time, jump over the table in his spurs and tuck into whatever food was going.

There are also tales of the king trying to interest Thomas in the joys of sex and of Thomas rejecting such pleasures as not being compatible with holy orders.

That may be no more than a story, but there is no evidence of Thomas ever having an amorous relationship or, for that matter, any really intimate relationship with anybody. For all the boisterousness of his friendship with the king, he seems to have been a very private person whose passion, in later life anyway, seems to have been centred in his relationship with God and the life to come.

But Thomas did not let his religious commitments get in the way of his duties as Royal Chancellor. His handling of 'the Great Scutage' is evidence of this.

Scutage (shieldage) was a tax which was levied as a substitute for providing the king with fully-armed knights. When Henry demanded one of these in 1159 to pay for his wars in France, the Church expected to be exempted from it, or at least to be allowed to avoid it. Thomas used his knowledge of the Church to make sure that, apart from one or two exceptions of his own choosing, it paid the tax in full. The Church saw this as a piece of gross ingratitude.

Thomas did not care. He was now the 'king's man' and all past loyalties were forgotten.

As the 'king's man', Thomas distinguished himself as a soldier. At the head of seven hundred knights of his own household he served valiantly in France.

Meanwhile Archbishop Theobald had grown old and feeble. He had felt Thomas's ingratitude over the Great Scutage very keenly but still believed he loved the Church at heart. He sent messages to France, begging Thomas to come and see him before he died, but Thomas did not come.

In 1161 Theobald died. The king let it be known that he wanted Thomas to be the new Archbishop of Canterbury. It was also known that Theobald had dearly wanted that too, but for different reasons.

During his lifetime Theobald had worked hard to gain privileges for the Church from Henry's predecessor, King Stephen. He thought Thomas was the man to protect these privileges. Henry, on the other hand, thought Thomas would help him to get them back.

The bishops, persuaded against their will, made no secret of their disappointment, while the monks were deeply offended. By tradition, the Archbishops of Canterbury were monks. Not only was Thomas not a monk, he was no more than a deacon, a king's clerk who had also been a soldier!

Thomas was not sure he should accept the office. He warned Henry that it could end their friendship, but the king took no notice and arranged for Thomas to be Royal Chancellor and Archbishop at the same time.

In the event, Theobald was right and Henry was wrong.

By becoming an archbishop, Thomas had changed masters again. He was 'God's man' now and all his previous loyalties were forgotten.

He soon resigned the office of Royal Chancellor, turned his back on the king's court and devoted himself to his religious duties and the interests of the Church.

Of course this led to confrontations between Thomas and the king. In one of these we see Thomas doing exactly the opposite of what he did for the king at the Great Scutage.

Henry had attempted to revive Sheriff's Aid. This was a small tax that used to be paid to the Sheriffs. Henry wanted it to be collected again and paid into his own treasury. Thomas blocked this and also declared that the Church would not pay a penny towards it.

Henry, who always liked to have his own way, summoned a Council of Bishops at Westminster. This council was called to discuss a small matter of precedence between the archbishoprics of Canterbury and York. But, as often happened at the kings's Councils, when they arrived the bishops found they were discussing something different, something for which they were not prepared.

King Henry started by demanding that 'criminous clerks' were to be handed over to the king's justice.

This would take away from the Church a valuable privilege that had been confirmed by King Stephen and the bishops refused.

The king then commanded them to do so, insisting that this was an Ancient Royal Custom (ie., one that existed before King Stephen's time).

Again the bishops, led by Thomas, refused.

The king then commanded each bishop to swear that he would observe the Ancient Royal Customs.

Each bishop affirmed that he would obey his king in all things: 'salvo ordine meo' . . . ('saving my order').

This meant that they would do whatever the king asked except anything that was against the laws of the Church.

At this the king lost his temper and stormed out of the council.

The next morning, still in a temper, Henry left London early but, before leaving, he demanded back from Thomas the estates that he had held as Chancellor. Some of the bishops, remembering that the king was their landlord too, went after him in a panic to make peace. The king received them gently and asked them to try to persuade Thomas to agree to observe the Royal Customs without reservation. He insisted that this was only a formality, a necessary confirmation of his power as king, and he assured them that the Constitutions would not be used against the Church.

So, eventually, Thomas was persuaded. He agreed, and later publicly swore, to observe the Ancient Royal Customs.

But what were these Customs?

It seems that nobody knew for sure.

Then Henry, having no doubt prepared the material beforehand, invited some senior lords to provide what was called a 'recognition' of the Ancient Royal Customs.

This was done at a Council held at the king's hunting lodge at Clarendon in Wiltshire. The document was called the Constitutions of Clarendon.

When Thomas and the bishops read it they were appalled. Among other restrictions the Constitutions forbade members of the Church to leave the country without the king's permission. That, in effect, cut them off from Europe and the Pope. They also removed the right of appeal to the Pope and established that no servant of the king could be excommunicated without his permission. The Constitutions regarding the treatment of 'criminous clerks' were not unreasonable. They were to be taken to the king's court and if it thought fit, handed over to the Church court. If they were then found guilty of a non Church-type crime they would lose the protection of the Church and be handed back to the king's court for sentence.

Whatever the bishops may have thought of the Constitutions, they assumed that because they had already sworn to observe the Ancient Royal Customs they had no alternative but to accept them and go home. Thomas did not. He refused to set his seal to the Constitutions and the Council broke up. The bishops were now completely confused. Some were very angry with Thomas for going back on his word, but none of them was as angry and ashamed as Thomas was with himself. He returned to Canterbury and did elaborate public penances, refusing to say Mass or serve at the altar, to show that by giving way to the king he had committed a terrible sin against the Church.

No doubt Thomas did this mainly to irritate the king but it also irritated the bishops and many others, including the Pope. He sent Thomas a letter absolving him from any sin he imagined he had committed and telling him to get on with his job.

Henry, thinking everything was settled, sent a copy of the Constitutions to the Pope for his approval.

The Pope, Alexander III, was living in France at the time because he was in exile from Rome. The Church

was 'in schism', that is: divided. There was another pope, Victor IV, supported by the Holy Roman Emperor Frederick 1st, waiting in Italy. So Alexander needed all the political support he could get from Henry II of England and Louis VII of France. Naturally enough, he was anxious not to offend either of them.

However, Alexander looked at the Constitutions and saw that Henry was trying to take the English Church out of his control. He recognized only six of the Constitutions and condemned the other ten.

This left the bishops in England in a difficult situation. They were, as they put it, between the hammer and the anvil—between the king's anger and the Pope's authority. Which could they obey without being punished by the other?

King Henry went ahead with one of his periodic 'sweeps', in which his officers rounded up criminals of all sorts, including the 'criminous clerks' of the Church, and brought them to justice.

Thomas responded by forbidding the trial of the Church's clerks by the king's justices on pain of being excommunicated if they disobeyed.

This put the king's justices in a difficult situation!

King Henry then called a Great Council at Northampton. There, by his command, Thomas was to answer a relatively minor charge of not turning up at some dispute about land. This matter was dealt with quite swiftly but the king then started listing charges of embezzlement and theft against Thomas, dating from when he was Chancellor.

These charges were obviously trumped up because when he became Archbishop Thomas was formally forgiven all his earthly obligations.

Thomas, not expecting this attack, had no case prepared and the king became more and more angry and threatening. In the end, Thomas declared that the king's court not only had no right to try him on a case without giving him a chance to prepare a defence, it had no right to try him at all. With that he left.

Having made plans in case something like that should happen, Thomas disappeared and made his way in disguise to France.

he journey to France was long, uncomfortable and sometimes dangerous. Eventually Thomas came to Sens, a city to the south-east of Paris, where Pope Alexander III had his court. He was received courteously into the Pope's protection, but the Pope could not do much to help him in his quarrel with Henry because of his own political troubles.

So, at the Pope's invitation, Thomas settled at the Cistercian Abbey of Pontigny, where he stayed for some years, receiving a stream of penniless relatives, friends and associates who had been booted out by Henry.

Thomas was made welcome by Louis VII of France, who gave him some help in his campaign to recover control of the English Church, but this help depended mainly on whether or not Louis was friends with Henry at that particular time.

The relationship of Louis and Henry seems a bit strange to us. Henry was at war with Louis and, quite often, it seems, dined with him. They admired and complimented each other on their prowess as soldiers and, from time to time, did battle for various disputed territories. This enmity did not stop Louis agreeing to the marriage of his daughter Margaret (a child) to Henry's son Prince Henry (a young boy).

In England everybody was thoroughly fed up with the long wrangle between Henry and Thomas. The way the state and the church worked together to run the country was something that had always been settled by careful negotiations. This could have happened in this case quite easily if Henry and Thomas had not been so proud and obstinate. The barons and bishops worked hard to find compromises and acceptable forms of words but to no avail. Both Thomas and Henry only wanted to win.

The history of Thomas's exile in France is thoroughly mixed up with international and Papal politics. The Pope constantly supported Thomas with one hand and regularly betrayed his support with the other. Thomas excommunicated his enemies from exile but this did not seem to have much effect. In the end it became clear that he was not going to make any progress with his campaign without the active, wholehearted, help of the Pope. He also realized that he would only get that help if Henry did something the Pope could not forgive.

In 1170 Henry did this.

Because he spent half of his time in his lands in France, Henry had long been aware of the need to have somebody to share his responsibilities and who would take over if anything happened to him. So, in June 1170, he had the Archbishop of York crown his eldest son, Prince Henry, King of England.

The Pope had already forbidden this.

Thomas, as Archbishop of Canterbury, had the sole right and duty to crown kings of England. So the coronation was not only illegal, it was an insult to him and a denial of his authority. Thomas had the right to ask the Pope to lay an 'interdict' on the whole of England as a punishment for such an act.

But Thomas did not want such a dreadful thing to happen to his own country, so before the coronation happened, he sent a very friendly letter to Roger of Pont-l'Eveque who was Archbishop of York, warning him that this could happen if he went ahead with it.

It was not easy to send letters to England at the time because Henry was blockading all the ports, but Thomas gave the letter to a nun who managed to smuggle it in and deliver it by hand to the Archbishop of York. He ignored it and crowned the young king.

By this time the Pope had returned to Italy and communications had become very slow. He was certainly going to be very angry indeed when he came to hear that the coronation had happened.

Louis VII was already angry with Henry. He was angry because his daughter Margaret, who was married to Prince Henry, had been robed for her coronation as his queen and then, at the last moment, been left behind in France.

It is not easy to see why Henry took the unwise action of going ahead with the illegal coronation or why he insulted Louis VII and his daughter in that unnecessary way. It is quite likely that he was just making a defiant gesture. Henry was a man of violent temper.

Nevertheless, Henry had certainly come to hear of the letter Thomas had sent to the Archbishop of York. He had also received the Pope's letter forbidding the coronation. Sensing perhaps that he had overstepped the mark he decided it was time to placate the Pope by making friends with Thomas again.

So Henry crossed to France in a peace-making mood. He met with Louis and made his peace with him. Then he arranged to meet Thomas at Freteval in Touraine.

Their meeting, which took place in a meadow near the town, was very emotional. The old friends greeted each other most affectionately and everything Thomas asked for was agreed to at once.

He was to be reinstated as archbishop and his lands and those of his banished friends and relations were to be returned. The king asked him to crown the young king and queen again in order to make it legal. Thomas said he would lift the excommunications and would serve Henry once again as archbishop.

They embraced and rejoiced that there was peace between them at last.

There seemed to be no end to their good will but, as can so easily happen, in their enthusiasm they had brushed aside their differences rather than solved them. After their meeting the king was slow to do his part and Thomas did not hesitate to nag him.

Now that Thomas was 'his man' again, Henry just wanted him to tag along with his court in France for a while but Thomas wanted to get back to England. They quarrelled again, and again were reconciled. Thomas again asked for the 'kiss of peace' which Henry had long refused. The 'kiss of peace' was a public affirmation of friendship that even an unscrupulous king like Henry would not dare to betray. Henry refused again.

In October 1170 Thomas received the Pope's response to the illegal coronation. This was severe and took the form of letters condemning the coronation and confirming Thomas's power as 'Legate of the Holy See'. These made him the Pope's direct agent, empowering him, in the Pope's name, to excommunicate and dismiss the bishops and any others who had taken part in the illegal coronation.

Thomas, who genuinely thought his long quarrel with the king was coming to an end at last, was reluctant to carry out these harsh sentences and wrote to the Pope for some gentler ones which he could use if all went well.

During the same month Thomas received news about Ranulf de Broc, one of the king's more hostile officers, whose family had taken over Thomas's estates in Kent when he left and now, far from restoring them, was carefully plundering them and carrying off the stock.

Thomas now asked the king to come back to England with him so that they could make a new start together. The king seemed to agree and Thomas got ready to leave for England. Then at the last moment Henry changed his mind. He left a curt note for Thomas informing him that he was going somewhere else in France. He did not send Thomas the money that he had promised but he did send John of Oxford, an old enemy who Thomas had once excommunicated, to conduct him through the blockade on the channel ports.

Thomas, now thoroughly angry, arranged for the Pope's original letters of excommunication to be smuggled into England and served on the guilty bishops at Dover. This done, he set sail for England. ·

It was just as well John of Oxford was with him because Ranulf de Broc and the Sheriff of Kent were waiting to arrest Thomas and his retinue as they landed at Sandwich.

John of Oxford overruled de Broc and Thomas came home to Canterbury at last. He received a great welcome in the city. But very soon the chaplains to the bishops, accompanied by Ranulf de Broc and the Sheriff of Kent came to him and demanded that for the sake of peace he should set aside the excommunications he had laid on the bishops, make peace with Roger, Archbishop of York and observe the Ancient Royal Customs!

Then Thomas made the decision that probably cost him his life.

He refused to lift the excommunications unless the bishops swore to obey all future commands of the Pope. He also declined to make his peace with Roger of York because, he said, Roger's fate was in the hands of the Pope, not in his.

When Roger of York heard this he decided to go to France and tell Henry what Thomas was up to.

Although Thomas had been received with rapture in Canterbury, his arrival was received with alarm by much of the rest of the country. All they had heard of Thomas was what Roger of York had told them. They saw him as the king's enemy and knew nothing of any reconciliation.

To allay their fears, Thomas started on a ceremonial tour through the country on his way to pay homage to the young king at Winchester, bringing him a rich present of fine horses. Thomas's procession was received by jubilant crowds in London—the merchants had always liked Thomas. He was one of their sons.

The young king, having been told by Roger of York that Thomas intended to condemn his coronation and depose him, sent word to Thomas that he would not receive him and commanded him to return to Canterbury and stay there.

Reluctantly Thomas did so. He returned to find that Canterbury was being blockaded, or rather pestered, by Ranulf de Broc, his nephew Robert and some other king's men who had profited by Thomas's exile.

Thomas felt angry and let down by his reception. On Christmas day he preached a sermon excommunicating the whole de Broc family for the 'final insult' of cutting off the tail of one of his pack-horses.

As he dashed the candles to the ground, Thomas's clerks and the monks may have felt that he was over-reacting to a minor practical joke, but Thomas was on the attack now and the de Brocs had been warned. He also included in his condemnation the bishops who had attended the illegal coronation, and that was serious!

Meanwhile Roger, Archbishop of York, and two of the bishops who had attended the illegal coronation, Gilbert of London and Jocelin of Salisbury, had travelled to Bures in Normandy where King Henry was celebrating Christmas with his court.

Gilbert and Jocelin could not be received by the king because they were excommunicated, so Roger had to tell the story.

It was a lie.

Roger described Thomas's procession from Canterbury as a small army and the happy crowds that had come to greet him as a vicious rabble. He said that they were making a circuit of the kingdom, terrorising the people with threats of violence and excommunication if they did not support him.

King Henry may not have taken theology seriously, but this sounded like insurrection, a threat to his power! He became enraged and made the famous speech in which he asked: "What idle treacherous knaves have I nourished in my court that they allow me to be shamefully mocked by a low-born clerk?"

The king does not seem to have either asked or commanded any of the idle knaves to get rid of Thomas. In fact, after he recovered his temper he and his council thought carefully and sensibly about what was to be done. They decided to send a deputation of high-ranking noblemen to Canterbury to invite Thomas to go with them to Winchester and swear obedience to the young king. This Thomas would almost certainly have been glad to do but, in the event, he did not get the chance.

Four of the king's barons, Reginald Fitzurse, Hugh de Moreville, William de Tracy and Richard le Bret, seem to have taken the king's words as a personal challenge. Or perhaps they may have taken some words of Roger of York, who gave them money for the journey.

Either way, without waiting for any decisions or deputations, they slipped away from Bures and took ship for England. They landed and made their way to the de Brocs' castle at Saltwood.

Early in the afternoon of December 29th, 1170, the four barons, with Ranulf and Robert de Broc and a company of knights and soldiers, rode into Canterbury. They posted men around the archbishop's palace and entered the courtyard. The four barons hung their armour on a mulberry tree and went into the palace.

They were received courteously and offered refreshment, which they refused. They were shown into Thomas's bedroom where he was talking with some of his clerks and officers. They sat there for a few moments until the archbishop spoke to them. They replied to his greeting in a surly manner and immediately started to argue with him. This was a foolish thing to do because Thomas was better at arguing and made them seem foolish and clumsy.

The barons commanded Thomas to go with them as their captive to Winchester to answer for his crimes before the young king. They probably did not know that Thomas had already tried to present himself to the young king and had been ordered back to Canterbury. No doubt he would have been pleased to go to Winchester as the young king's guest, but he certainly was not willing to be taken there as a prisoner to be tried for crimes he did not recognize.

Soon they all became enraged, especially after Thomas reminded the barons that three of them had been his 'vassals' and had sworn oaths of obedience to him when he was Chancellor.

Finally the barons could take no more. They jumped up and, in the name of the king, commanded Thomas's clerks to hold him until they came back. Thomas laughed scornfully and said he would be waiting.

Then the barons stormed out of the palace, intending to put on their armour and return to arrest Thomas.

Unfortunately that did not work out. Two of Thomas's servants slammed and barred the front door.

Furious, the barons beat on the door while, inside the palace, Thomas's clerks and monks were scuttling about like frightened chickens.

Thomas, it seems, was excited but not in a panic. He may have had some idea that his life might be in danger but there is no evidence that the barons intended to kill him. Thomas knew that the barons were not really of a high enough rank to command an archbishop, so he probably looked on their behaviour as a piece of impertinence to be treated with contempt.

Even if he had thought his life was in danger, it is doubtful whether he would have minded. He had been a distinguished and fearless soldier in his time and now he was an archbishop. Like all priests in the twelfth century he truly believed that to be a martyr, to be killed in the service of God, was a glorious end to a holy life, something to be hoped for, not feared. Death, although painful perhaps, was just the gateway to Heaven and the life to come.

He had also told the barons that he would wait for them in the palace and he was going to stay there.

Having failed to break down the door, Robert de Broc led the barons round to the back of the palace. There they climbed on to a roof and began to break down a wooden partition.

It was clearly only a matter of minutes before they would come pouring in.

So Thomas's monks and clerks picked him up bodily and carried him down through the cellars of the palace and out into the cathedral cloisters.

"After all," they said, "It is time for the archbishop to attend the evening service of Vespers."

In the cloisters they managed to form a procession and, led by his cross, they half-shoved the reluctant priest into the north-west transept of the cathedral.

They went to close the door but Thomas told them not to, saying that this was a church, not a castle.

The barons could be heard running through the cloisters. When they reached the door to the cathedral they probably paused. This was a holy place.

Then Reginald Fitzurse stepped forward and shouted: ''Where is the traitor Thomas Becket?''

Naturally nobody answered that. So he shouted again: ''Where is the archbishop?''

Then Thomas stepped forward and replied: ''Here I am, no traitor but a priest of God.''

Then the barons marched in and confronted Thomas, commanding him to come with them to Winchester to be tried by the young king. Once again he refused and another shouting-match developed.

There is some confusion about what was said in the darkness of the cathedral but what happened was recorded by no less than four eye-witnesses.

The barons realized, even in the heat of their anger, that to attack Thomas in the Cathedral, which was consecrated ground, would be a mortal sin. So they tried to lift him on to the back of William de Tracy, who was not wearing armour and so was not weighed down with ironmongery. Their intention was to carry him out of the holy place and take him prisoner.

They did not succeed.

Thomas had been a soldier. He was also very angry himself, and probably outraged at being continually picked up and carried about like a parcel. He grabbed Reginald Fitzurse, called him a foul name and threw him to the ground. A brawl followed, during which Thomas must at some point have realized that he had come to the end of his earthly road, because he knelt and, murmuring a prayer, was struck such a blow by Richard le Bret that his sword cut the whole top off Thomas's head and was smashed to pieces on the floor.

''Royeau! Royeau!' (''The King! The King!''), shouted the barons as they rushed out of the cathedral.

Then perhaps they may have had doubts about whether Thomas was really dead, because one of their number, a clerk dressed as a soldier, called Hugh of Horsea, ran back and stuck the point of his sword into Thomas's skull, spreading brains and blood all over the stones.

''That fellow will not rise again!'' he shouted.

It is said that as the barons and their men rode away from the archbishop's palace with their saddle-bags crammed with Thomas's treasure, a great storm broke over the city. The sky over the desecrated cathedral turned purple as the terrified townspeople crept back to dip fragments of cloth in the blood of the martyr.

Not all those present saw Thomas as a holy martyr. Many of the monks of Canterbury had always been hostile to Thomas. Not without reason they had seen him as a clerk who had reached high office through the favour of the king and, having been foolish enough to defy his master, had got no more than he deserved.

Robert de Broc came back a short while later and told the monks that if they didn't get rid of the body quickly, he would have it dragged around the town as a common thief and thrown on the dump.

We can wonder how different the history of England and the Church might have been if that had happened. Although the great King's Clerk would surely have had some place in history, there might have been no 'holy blissful martyr' in Canterbury for the pilgrims to seek and none of their rich gifts for the Church to enjoy.

Although Thomas was dead, he had not lost the game. He had another card up his sleeve, as one might say. A card that could only be played after he was dead.

However much they felt that Thomas was to blame for his own fate, the monks did not want him to be buried without honour. So they carried his body into the crypt of the cathedral.

There Robert of Merton, Thomas's Confessor, stripped the body in preparation for burial.

Beneath the Archbishop's outer garments he revealed the monk's habit that Thomas had worn at Pontigny. This showed them that Thomas had been a monk after all. He was one of them!

That caused them great joy. But it was nothing to the joy they felt when the monk's habit was removed and they saw that Thomas was wearing a hair shirt and pants.

These extraordinarily scratchy garments were worn by holy people to make themselves even more holy by making themselves even more uncomfortable—mortifying the flesh it was called.

Thomas's flesh was exceptionally mortified because the hair shirt and pants were heavily infested with lice and fleas, so heavily that, as the body cooled, they trooped away in such numbers that, as one observer put it, it was like watching the top of a boiling cauldron.

This revolting revelation confirmed beyond a shadow of doubt that Thomas and everything about him was utterly holy. The news spread swiftly through the land and thousands flocked to Canterbury to touch his holy relics and pray for miracles at his tomb.

The restrictions in the Constitutions of Clarendon were forgotten and the Church remained secure in its powers and privileges. Thomas had won, and in due course he was made a saint.

There is no doubt that King Henry deeply regretted what had happened. Thomas had been his friend. He had said angry words when he was in a temper but he had not wanted his friend to be murdered. He had wanted him to be taken to Winchester.

Henry grieved deeply and took to himself the blame for what had happened. Four years later he came to Canterbury barefoot, to be scourged by a hundred or so monks and bishops as a penance for his part in the murder.

The blood of the martyr, said to be imbued with the power to work miracles, remained miraculously available, apparently in unlimited quantities, because pilgrims came from all over the world to pray at the martyr's tomb and buy little phials of blood and holy water. Over the next three and a half centuries the stream of pilgrims must have numbered hundreds of thousands, if not millions, of souls, many of whom brought rich gifts and offerings to the Church. So rich were these gifts that the power and wealth of the English Church for the next three hundred years was copiously nourished by this Medieval tourist trade.

Erasmus, the Dutch Theologian, came to Canterbury in 1526. He saw the wooden lid lifted off the marvellous gold and jewelled tomb and was shocked at the sheer richness of the place. He made the outrageous suggestion that a more Christian use of all that wealth would be to sell it and give the money to the poor.

But Erasmus did not know that the enormous wealth did not come from the Christian holiness of the great King's Clerk, but from the blessed presence of the fleas.

Perhaps, if he had known this, Erasmus would have thought the display more appropriate, because Thomas had loved grandeur and his house had always been magnificent.

AUTHORS' NOTE

The practice of making a continuous picture to illustrate a narrative must be as old as history. In fact it was probably one of the earliest ways of telling a story.

The idea for this one came to us when we were making a sound-recording of the appalling story of Thomas Becket for the Dean and Chapter of Canterbury Cathedral. The story called out for pictures but very few authentic pictures were available, certainly not enough to provide a consistent visual accompaniment to the sound-track. Naomi said: "well of course, if this were the twelfth century, we would spend the next few years sewing a Bayeux Tapestry of the story."

That was meant as a joke but it soon dawned on us that the idea was worth thinking about. A proper tapestry was a bit too much like hard work but, come to think of it, if they had had good paper and acrylic paint in the twelfth century they probably would have used that rather than needles and thread.

The idea began to seem less far-fetched when we thought of the potential a narrative frieze would have today. It would not only provide pictures for an audio-visual programme, it would also make a book, perhaps a film and video-cassettes and, finally, like the Bayeux Tapestry, it would continue to exist.

So the idea took root and very quickly gave forth a lot of pieces of paper which, when joined together with sticky-tape, formed a sort of barbaric comic strip, in a style that comes from somewhere between James Thurber and the Medieval illuminators.

We took the sketches to Dan Grisewood of Grisewood and Dempsey and said: "Book?"

Dan said "Yes. Go away and do it."

So we did.

It took Oliver nearly a year to paint the sixty-foot long illumination. A competent graphic artist could probably have done it in a quarter of the time but, apart from a spell at art school in 1943, Oliver's only experience in that field was a couple of short seasons as stage-manager cum scene-painter in long defunct weekly repertory companies.

So now the book is made. We hope you enjoy it. The various other incarnations are on their way but at this moment we don't know exactly where the long frieze will eventually come to roost.

We hope it will be possible to set it up somewhere, perhaps in Canterbury, where people can come and look at it and listen to the story. If that happens we hope you will come and see it. The publishers will probably know where it is.

Naomi Linnell.
Oliver Postgate.
August 1988.